Four rules of maths 6–7

Author: Lynn Huggins-Cooper
Illustrators: Emma Holt and Chris McGhie

How to use this book

Look out for these features!

IN THE ACTIVITIES

The parents' notes at the top of each activity will give you:
- ▶ a simple explanation about what your child is learning
- ▶ an idea of how you can work with your child on the activity.

This small page number guides you to the back of the book, where you will find further ideas for help.

These magic stars provide useful facts and helpful hints!

AT THE BACK OF THE BOOK

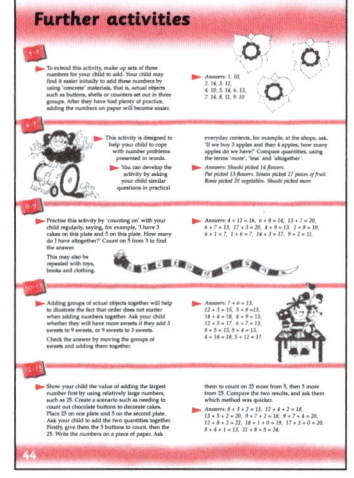

Every activity has a section for parents containing:
- ▶ further explanations about what the activity teaches
- ▶ games that can be easily recreated at home
- ▶ questions to ask your child to encourage their learning
- ▶ tips on varying the activity if it seems too easy or too difficult for your child.

You will also find the answers at the back of the book.

HELPING YOUR CHILD AS THEY USE THIS BOOK

Why not try starting at the beginning of the book and work through it? Your child should only attempt one activity at a time. Remember, it is best to learn little and often when we are feeling wide awake!

EQUIPMENT YOUR CHILD WILL NEED

- ▶ a pencil for writing
- ▶ an eraser for correcting mistakes
- ▶ coloured pencils for drawing and colouring in.

You might also like to have ready some spare paper and some collections of objects (for instance, small toys, Lego bricks, buttons...) for some of the activities.

Contents

Addition – more than 3 numbers

Add the numbers on the petals together.
Write the total in the centre.

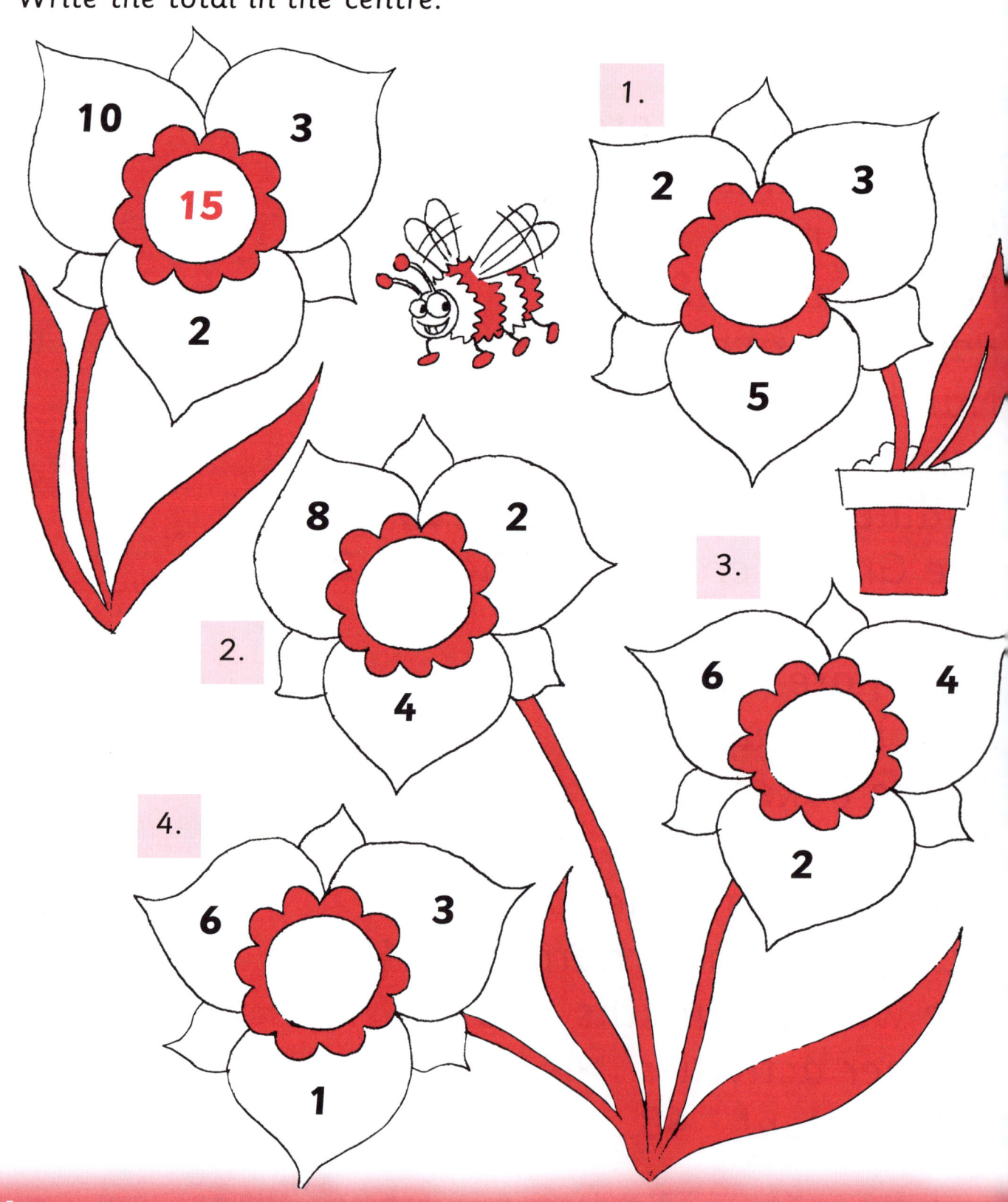

5.

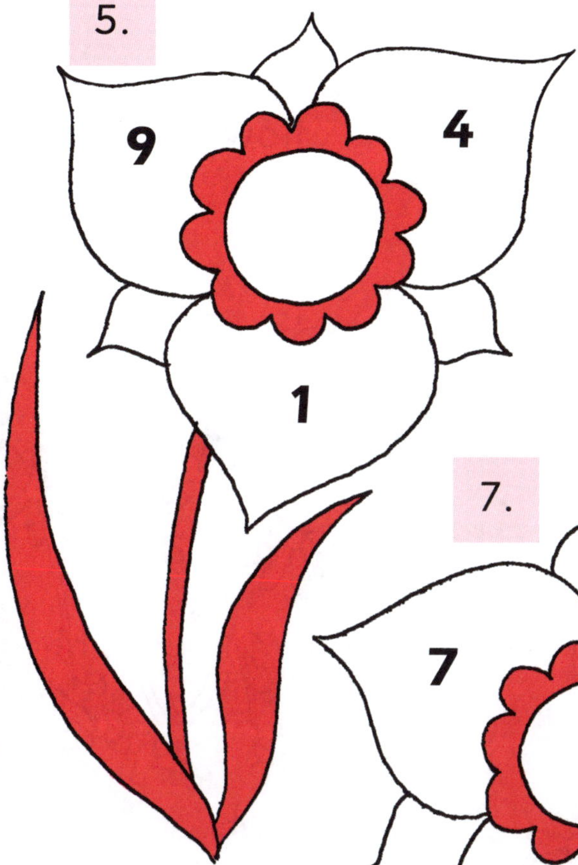

9 4

1

6.

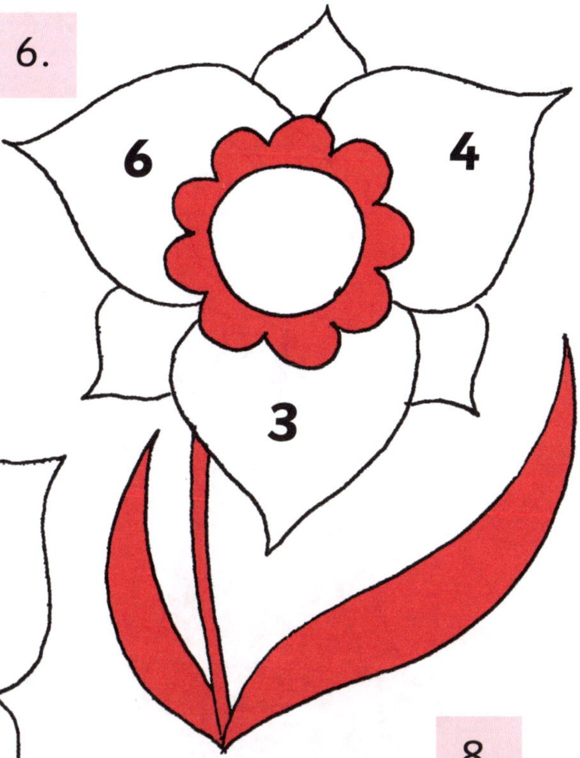

6 4

3

7.

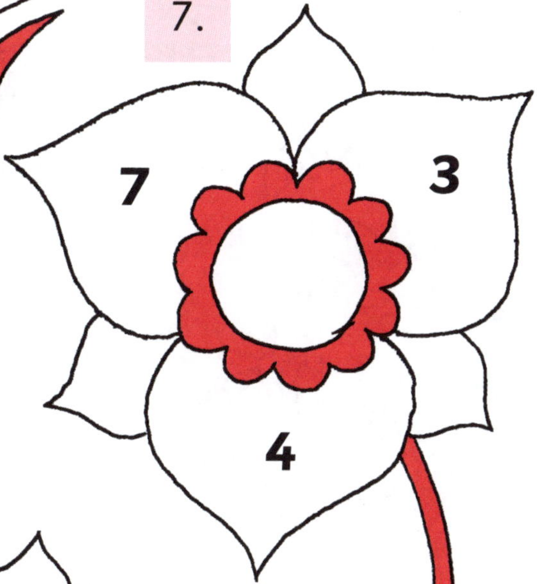

7 3

4

8.

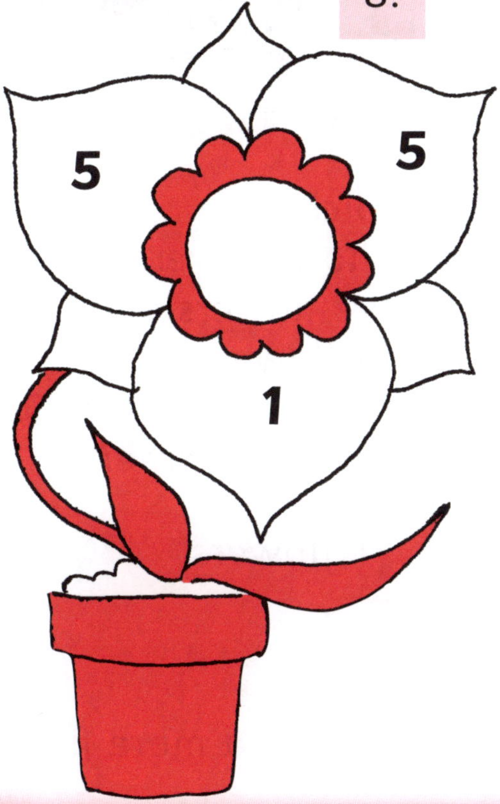

5 5

1

9.

9 1

0

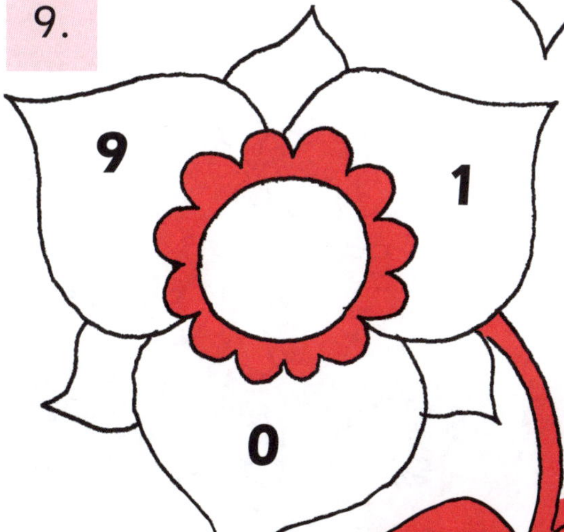

Word problems

Shushi picked 3 red flowers, 5 blue flowers
and 6 yellow flowers.
How many flowers did she pick altogether? ☐ flowers

Pat picked
6 yellow flowers,
5 blue flowers and
2 red flowers.
How many flowers did
he pick altogether?

☐ flowers

Who picked more flowers, Shushi or Pat? ☐

▶ This activity will help your child to add and compare quantities using word problems.

▶ Talk about the problems using 'more' and 'less'.

Parents

44

Simon picked
4 apples,
10 pears and
13 strawberries.
How many did he
pick altogether?

☐ fruits

Rosie picked
3 cabbages,
12 carrots and
5 potatoes.
How many did
she pick altogether?

☐ vegetables

Counting on

You can find the answer to these sums by 'counting on' from the first number. If you have 7 + 5, say '7' then count on 5 more, '8, 9, 10, 11, 12'.

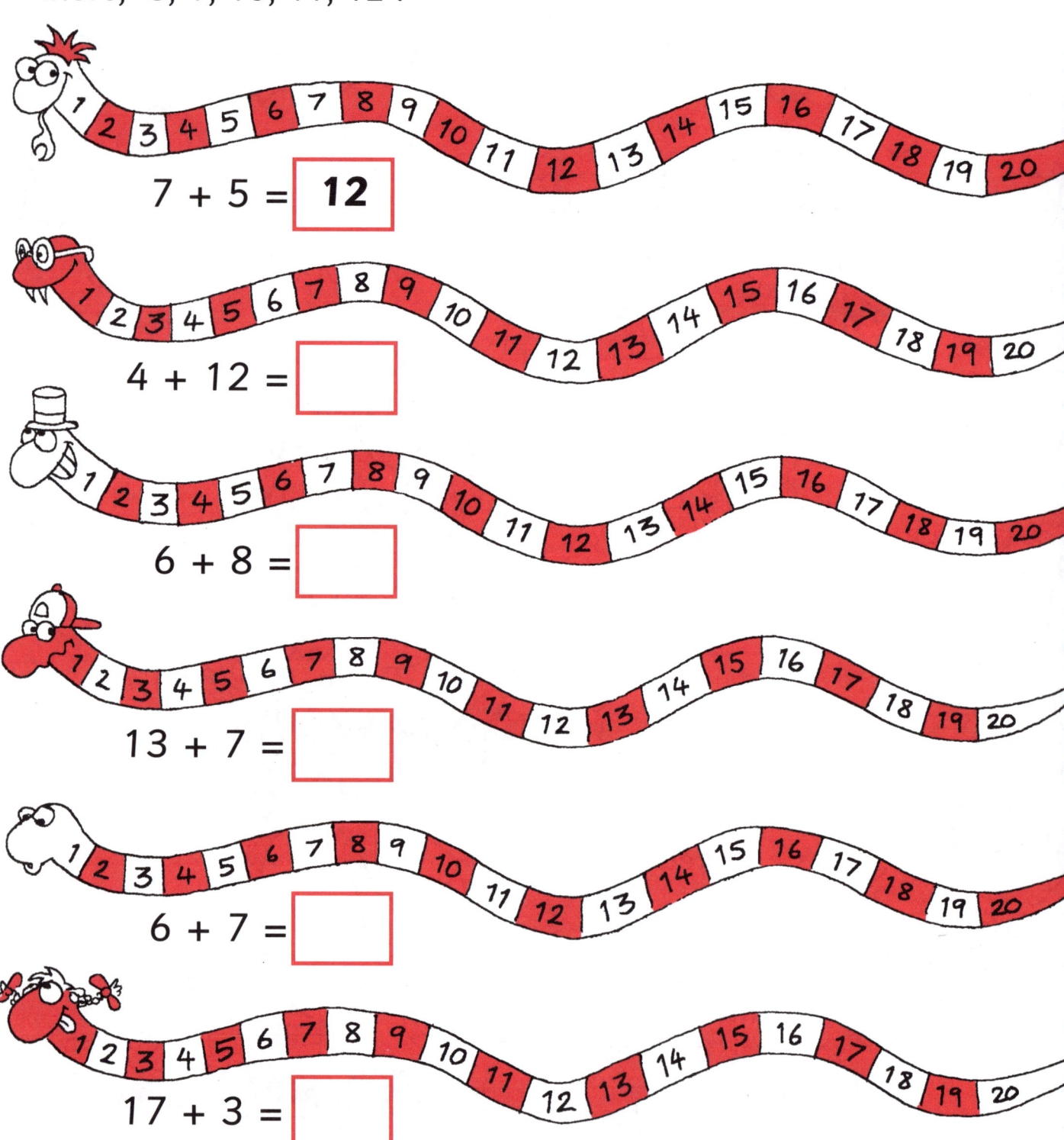

7 + 5 = 12

4 + 12 =

6 + 8 =

13 + 7 =

6 + 7 =

17 + 3 =

This activity will help your child to count on from given numbers to find an addition total.

Follow the count on the snakes with your fingers as your child works.

Parents

44

4 + 9 = ☐

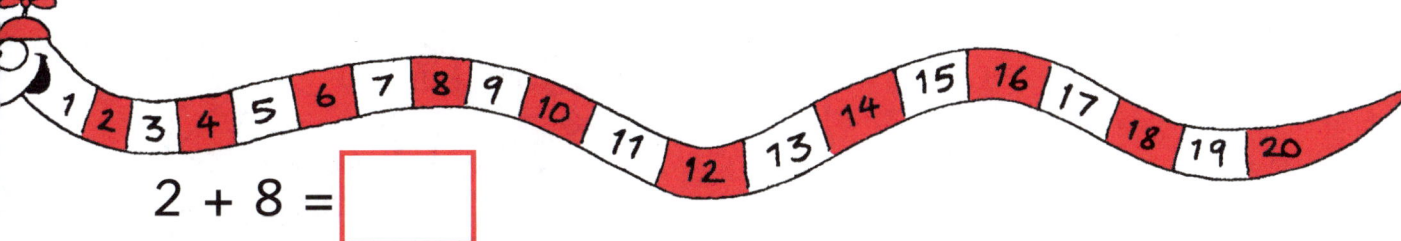

2 + 8 = ☐

6 + 1 = ☐

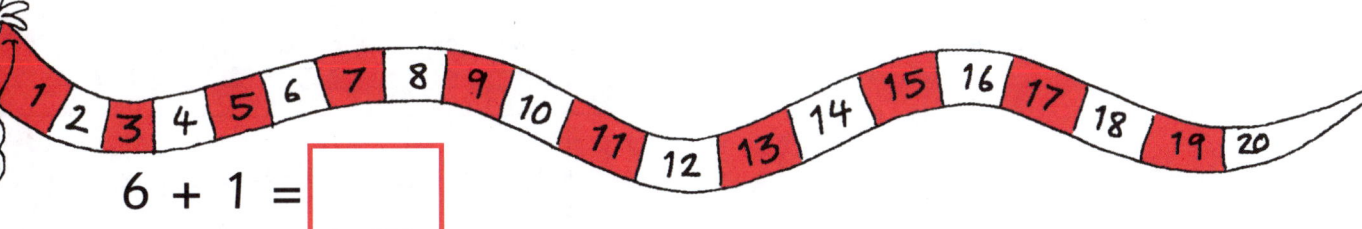

1 + 6 = ☐

14 + 3 = ☐

9 + 2 = ☐

Addition in any order

Kevin is using cards to do some addition sums.
Write the answers for him.

7 + 6 = ☐

12 + 3 = ☐

5 + 8 = ☐

14 + 4 = ☐

4 + 9 = ☐

12 + 5 = ☐

Oh no! Kevin has dropped the cards and the numbers are in a different order. Can you help him to answer them?

6 + 7 = ☐

3 + 12 = ☐

8 + 5 = ☐

9 + 4 = ☐

4 + 14 = ☐

5 + 12 = ☐

Did the order of the numbers matter?
Were the answers the same or different?

11

Largest numbers first

Look at the sets of three numbers. Write the largest in the giant's footstep. Then add the smaller numbers to it by counting on.

largest number

$3 + 2 + 8 =$ 8 $+$ 3 $+$ 2 $=$ 13

$12 + 2 + 4 =$ ___ $+$ ___ $+$ ___ $=$ 18

$5 + 2 + 13 =$ ___ $+$ ___ $+$ ___ $=$ 20

$7 + 9 + 2 =$ ___ $+$ ___ $+$ ___ $=$ ___

$4 + 7 + 9 =$ ___ $+$ ___ $+$ ___ $=$ ___

Finding the largest number, then counting on, will help your child to carry out mental arithmetic calculations quickly.

Help your child to identify the largest number first.

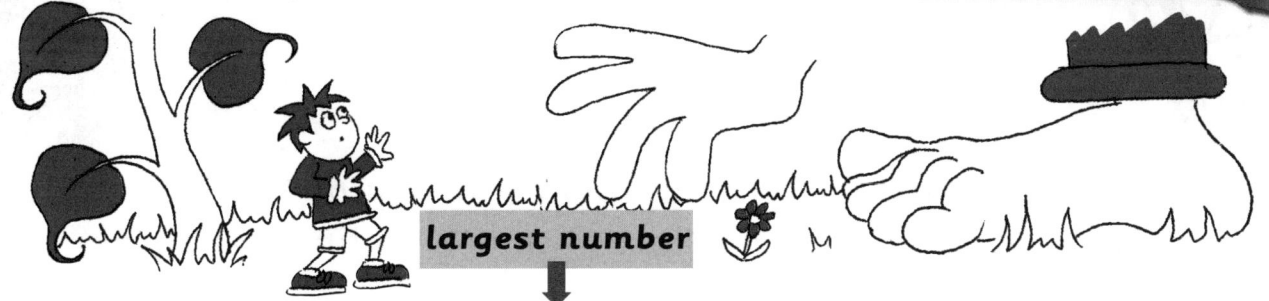

largest number

12 + 2 + 8 = ⬜ + ⬜ + ⬜ = ⬜

1 + 0 + 18 = ⬜ + ⬜ + ⬜ = ⬜

3 + 17 + 0 = ⬜ + ⬜ + ⬜ = ⬜

4 + 1 + 8 = ⬜ + ⬜ + ⬜ = ⬜

5 + 8 + 11 = ⬜ + ⬜ + ⬜ = ⬜

13

Pairs to make 10

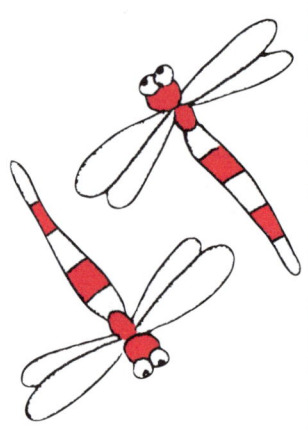

Look for two numbers that equal 10.
Then add the third number to find the total.

1 2 + 3 + 8 ➡ 2 + 8 = 10

Then add the number
left over, so ➡ 10 + 3 = 13

2 5 + 4 + 6 ➡ ☐ + ☐ = 10

Add the number
left over ➡ 10 + ☐ = ☐

3 5 + 9 + 5 ➡ ☐ + ☐ = 10

Add the number
left over ➡ 10 + ☐ = ☐

4 3 + 8 + 7 ➡ ☐ + ☐ = 10

Add the number
left over ➡ 10 + ☐ = ☐

Finding pairs of numbers that make 10 will help your child to calculate mentally quickly.

Help your child find the pairs before adding the third number.

5 4 + 9 + 1 = ☐ + ☐ = 10

Add the number left over ➡ 10 + ☐ = ☐

6 0 + 10 + 6 ➡ ☐ + ☐ = 10

Add the number left over ➡ 10 + ☐ = ☐

7 3 + 2 + 8 ➡ ☐ + ☐ = 10

Add the number left over ➡ 10 + ☐ = ☐

8 8 + 9 + 1 ➡ ☐ + ☐ = 10

Add the number left over ➡ 10 + ☐ = ☐

9 4 + 8 + 6 ➡ ☐ + ☐ = 10

Add the number left over ➡ 10 + ☐ = ☐

Pairs to make 20

Find the missing numbers to make each pair add up to 20!

1.

8 + ☐   7 + ☐

11 + ☐

10 + ☐

9 + ☐

2.

0 + ☐

3 + ☐

4 + ☐

1 + ☐

5 + ☐

2 + ☐

6 + ☐

Learning pairs of numbers that total 20 will help your child with mental calculations.

Help your child by counting on if they find this difficult.

3.

14 +

12 +

13 +

16 +

17 +

15 +

4.

19 +

18 +

20 +

Pairs to make 100

Find the numbers to make each pair add up to 100.

10 + ☐

0 + ☐

20 + ☐

100 + ☐

70 + ☐

50 + ☐

▷ Learning pairs of multiples of 10 that total 100 will help your child with mental arithmetic.

▷ Remind them what 'multiple of 10' means.

Parents

45

40 + ☐

90 + ☐

30 + ☐

80 + ☐

60 + ☐

Number stories

Here are some creepy-crawly stories to work out!
4 spiders were sitting in the sun when 3 more spiders
came along to play. That made 7 spiders altogether.

4 spiders + 3 spiders = | 7 | **spiders**

Then it started to rain and 3 spiders ran away.
How many spiders were left?

Watch out for the minus sign!

7 spiders – 3 spiders = [ ] **spiders**

Now complete these sums, and make up
a number story to tell.

6 snails + 5 snails = [ ] **snails**

11 snails – 5 snails = [ ] **snails**

Number stories will help your child relate numbers to real life.

Point out the connection between the pairs of calculations – that one undoes the other.

Parents

45

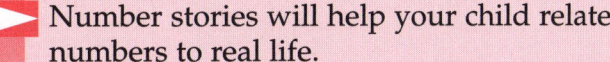

9 centipedes + 1 centipede ☐ centipedes

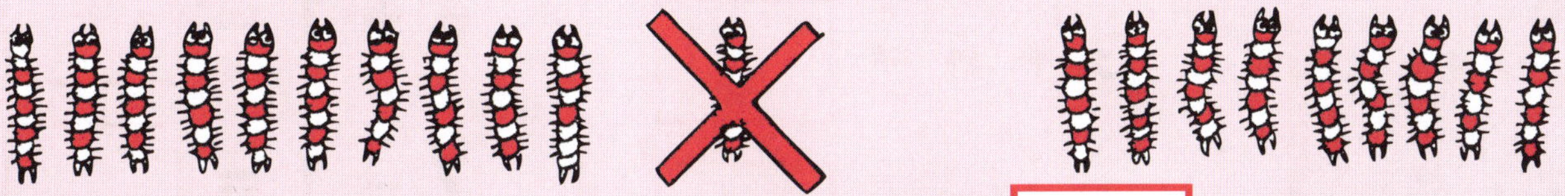

10 centipedes – 1 centipede ☐ centipedes

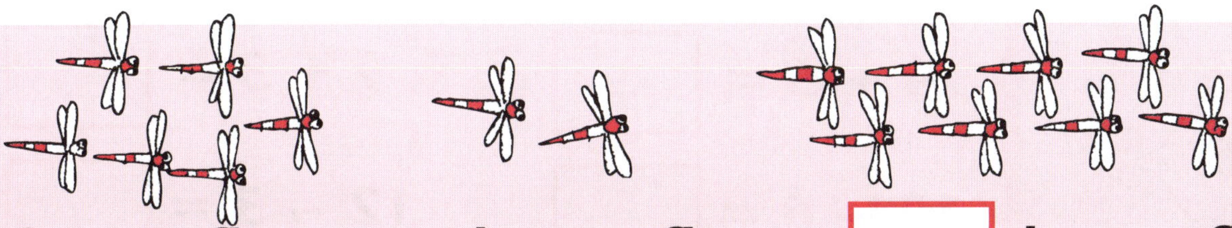

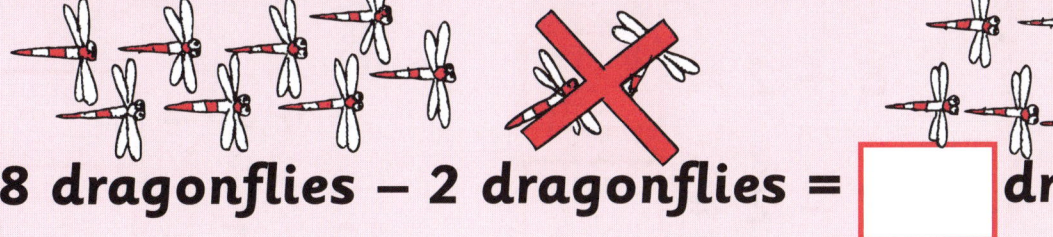

6 dragonflies + 2 dragonflies = ☐ dragonflies

8 dragonflies – 2 dragonflies = ☐ dragonflies

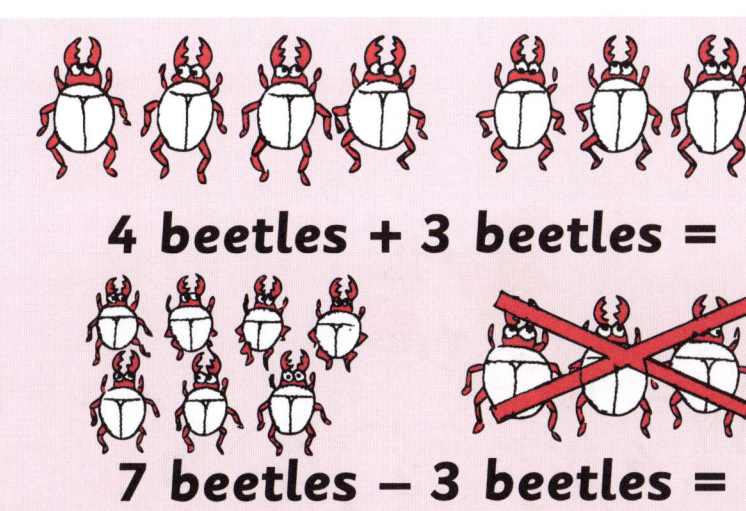

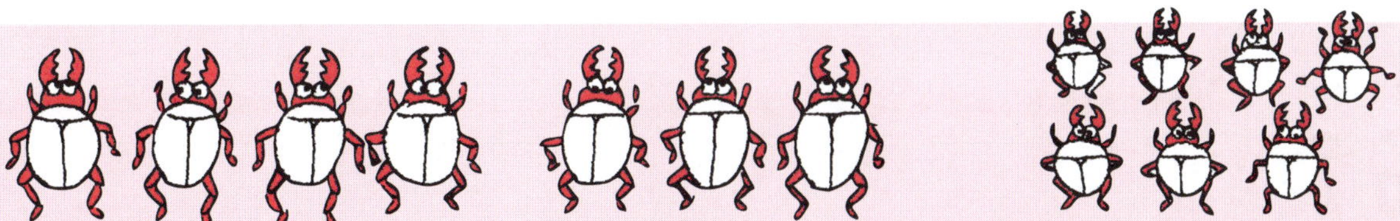

4 beetles + 3 beetles = ☐ beetles

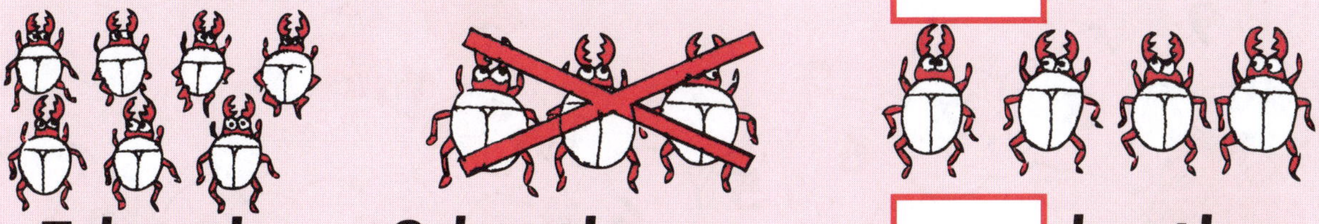

7 beetles – 3 beetles = ☐ beetles

Turn it around

Work these out. Use the beanstalks to help you to count forwards and backwards.

3 + 6 =

9 – 6 =

6 + 1 =

7 – 1 =

4 + 6 =

10 – 6 =

9 + 3 =

12 – 3 =

5 + 2 =

7 – 2 =

7 + 5 =

12 – 5 =

Beanstalk numbers: 20 19 18 17 16 15 14 13 12 11 10 9 8 7 6 5 4 3 2 1 0

This activity will help your child to see addition and subtraction as 'inverse operations'.

Use the beanstalk number lines to help them to work out their answers.

Parents

45

15 + 5 = ☐

20 – 5 = ☐

13 + 7 = ☐

20 – 7 = ☐

11 + 6 = ☐

17 – 6 = ☐

19 + 1 = ☐

20 – 1 = ☐

14 + 3 = ☐

17 – 3 = ☐

12 + 4 = ☐

16 – 4 = ☐

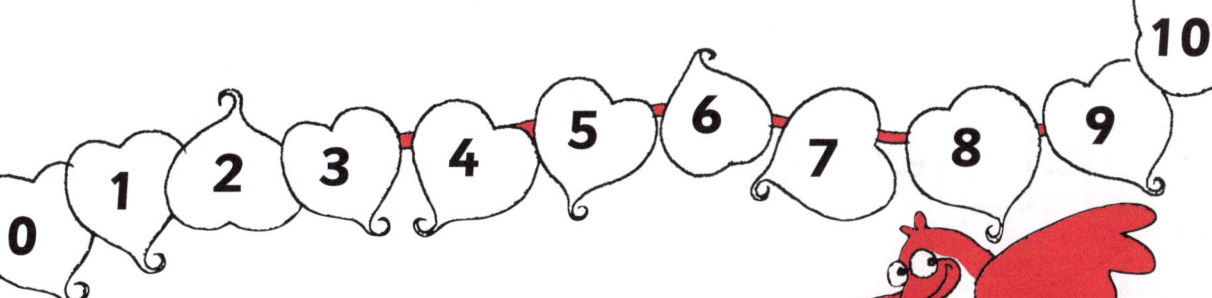

Adding and subtracting

Look at these.

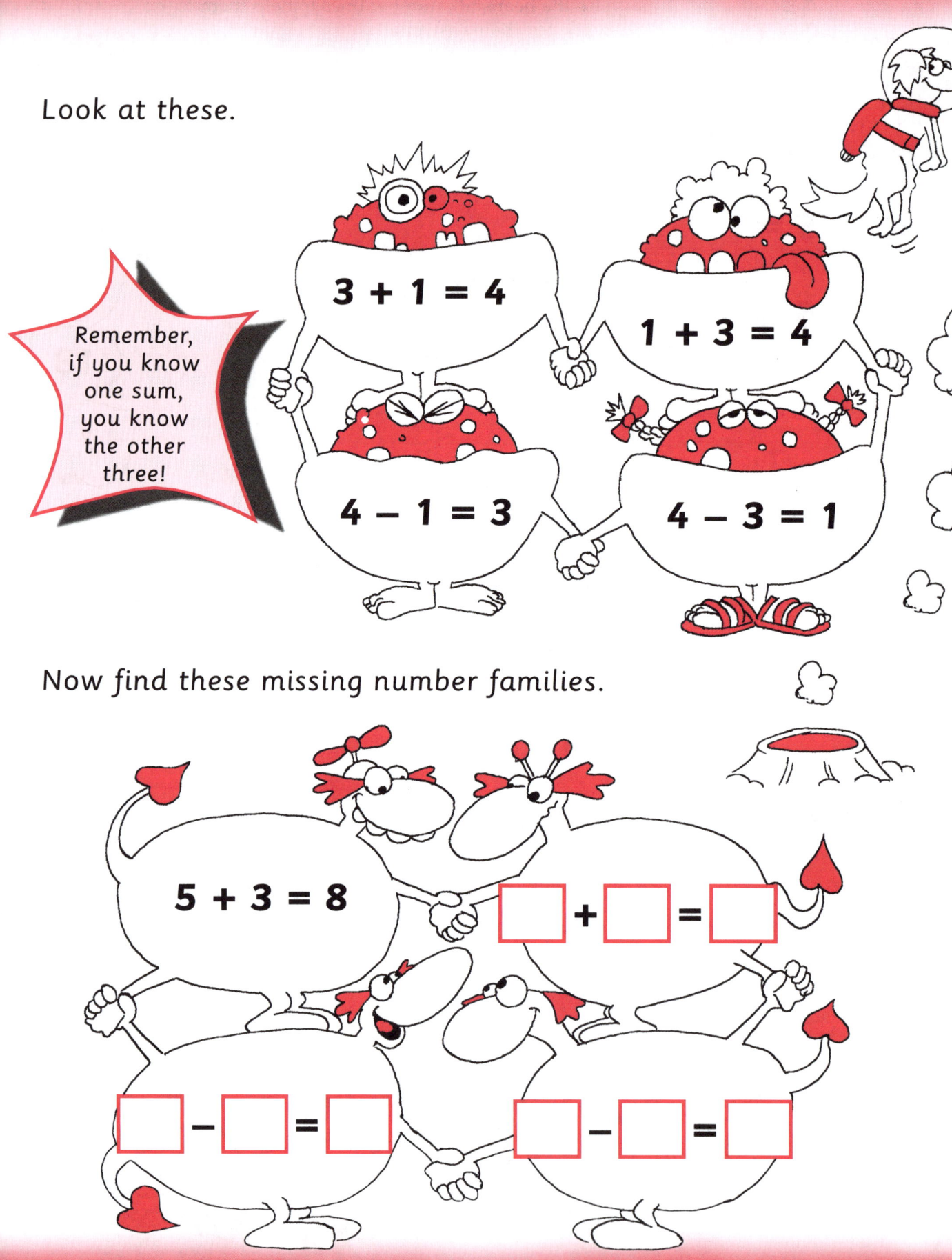

Remember, if you know one sum, you know the other three!

3 + 1 = 4

1 + 3 = 4

4 − 1 = 3

4 − 3 = 1

Now find these missing number families.

5 + 3 = 8

☐ + ☐ = ☐

☐ − ☐ = ☐

☐ − ☐ = ☐

This activity will help your child to develop their own mental strategies for solving problems.

Point out that all four statements have the same three numbers.

Parents

46

6 + 9 = 15

□ + □ = □

□ − □ = □

□ − □ = □

14 + 5 = 19

□ + □ = □

□ − □ = □

□ − □ = □

25

The Great Zero Game Show!

Look at what happens when 0 is **added** to a number. Does it make a difference?

12 TV sets + 0 TV sets = 12 TV sets

15 toys + 0 toys = 15 toys

Now do these sums.

18 computer games + 0 computer games = ☐
18 + 0 = ☐   games

24 boxes of chocolates + 0 boxes of chocolates = ☐
24 + 0 = ☐   boxe

30 colouring sets + 0 colouring sets = ☐ sets
30 + 0 = ☐

This activity will show your child that adding or subtracting 0 does not change a number.

Read through both sets of questions to help your child with the language.

Parents

46

Look at what happens when 0 is **taken away**, or **subtracted**, from a number. Does it make a difference?

12 TV sets – 0 TV sets = 12 TV sets

15 toys – 0 toys = 15 toys

Do these sums.

18 computer games – 0 computer games = ☐

18 – 0 = ☐ games

24 boxes of chocolates – 0 boxes of chocolates = ☐

24 – 0 = ☐ boxes

30 colouring sets – 0 colouring sets = ☐ sets

30 – 0 = ☐

27

Division as sharing

18

Colour in half the sweets in each bag in the border.

Now try these.

$18 \div 2 = \boxed{}$

$10 \div 2 = \boxed{}$

$24 \div 2 = \boxed{}$

$6 \div 2 = \boxed{}$

6

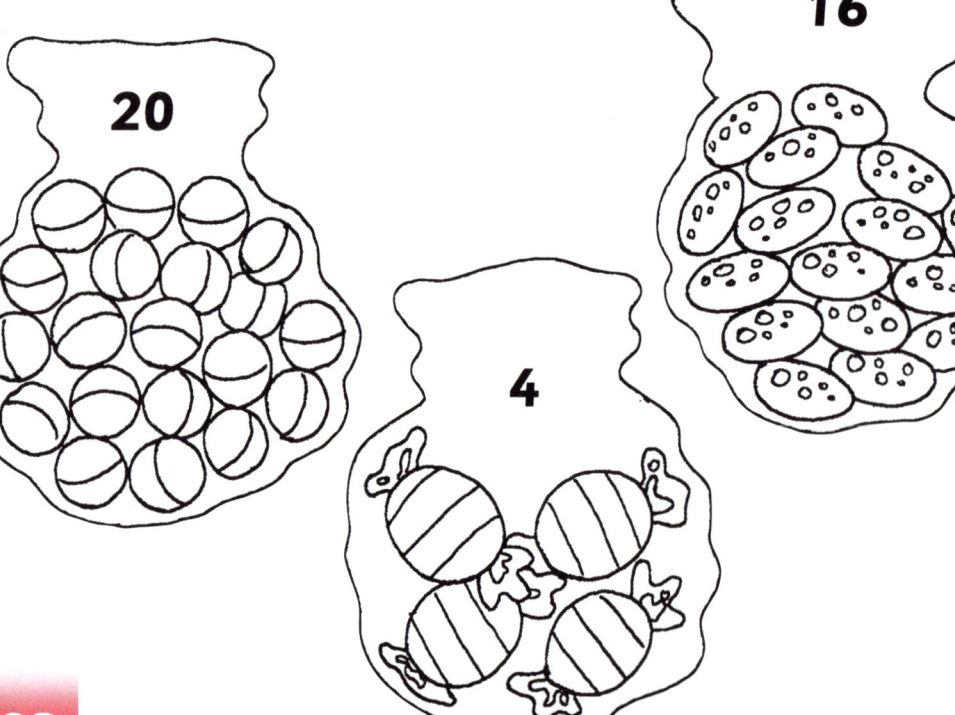

20

16

4

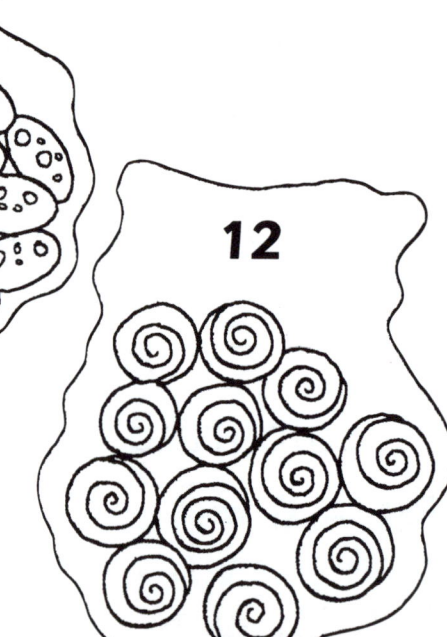

12

8 ÷ 2 = ☐

12 ÷ 2 = ☐

14 ÷ 2 = ☐

10 ÷ 2 = ☐

16 ÷ 2 = ☐

18

8

Choose a bag of sweets from the border.
If you share them equally between you and
a friend, how many will you each get?

2

18

10

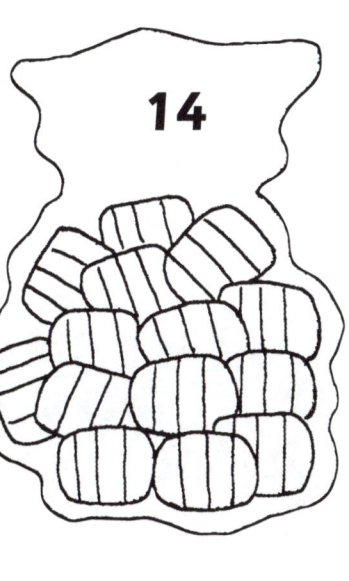

14

Fair share

Match the labels to the baskets.

4 groups of 3 eggs

3 groups of 4 eggs

6 groups of 2 eggs

5 groups of 2 eggs

▶ This will help your child to prepare for division calculations by finding sets of items.

▶ Help them to count the groups of items and match them to the labels.

Parents

46

2 groups of 3 eggs

2 groups of 6 eggs

2 groups of 5 eggs

3 groups of 2 eggs

Split them up

If there are 6 hamsters and 2 go in each cage, how many cages do we need?

6 ÷ 2 = ☐

If there are 20 crayons and 5 go in each pot, how many pots will we need?

20 ÷ 5 = ☐

If there are 16 lollies and 2 go in each party bag, how many bags are needed?

16 ÷ 2 = ☐

There are 15 spiders. If 3 spiders fit on each cobweb, how many cobwebs will there be?

$15 \div 3 =$ ☐

There are 18 boots. If each person has six boots, how many people are there?

$18 \div 6 =$ ☐

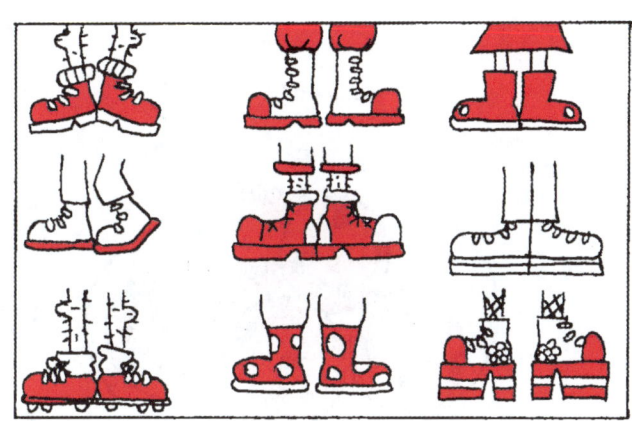

Now try these:

$12 \div 2 =$ ☐ $25 \div 5 =$ ☐

$15 \div 3 =$ ☐ $18 \div 3 =$ ☐

$9 \div 3 =$ ☐ $24 \div 3 =$ ☐

At the bakers

There are 3 cream horns in a box.
How many are there in 3 boxes?

3 + 3 + 3 = ☐

A shorter way to write this is:

3 x 3 = ☐

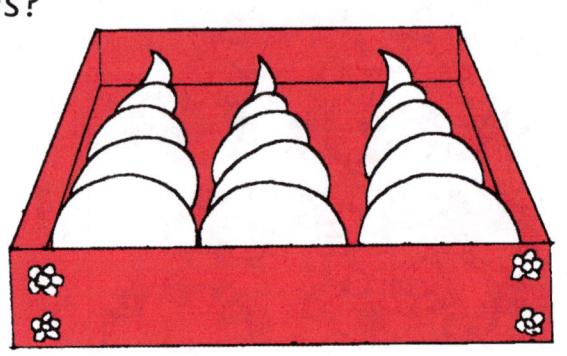

There are 5 chocolate chip cookies
in a bag. How many are in 4 bags?

5 + 5 + 5 + 5 = ☐

Written the shorter way:

5 x 4 = ☐

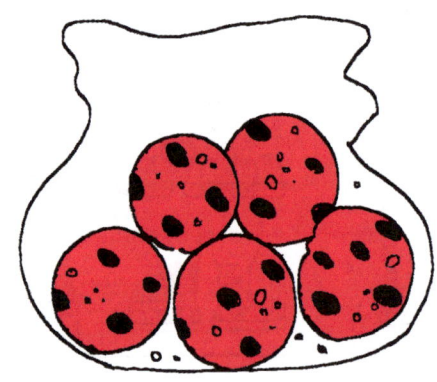

There are 6 buns in a pack.
How many are there in 3 packs?

6 + 6 + 6 = ☐

Written the shorter way:

☐

HARRY'S
— BUN SHOP —

There are 4 doughnuts in a box.
How many are in 3 boxes?

4 + 4 + 4 = ☐

Written the shorter way:

☐

Now try these multiplications. Write the 'shorter way' for each, using the multiplication sign 'x', and write the answer.

5 + 5 + 5 = ☐

Shorter way: ☐

3 + 3 + 3 + 3 + 3 = ☐

Shorter way: ☐

6 + 6 + 6 + 6 = ☐

Shorter way: ☐

4 + 4 + 4 + 4 + 4 + 4 + 4 = ☐

Shorter way: ☐

The 2 times table

When you learn your table facts, learn them using multiplication and division facts:

1 x 2 = 2		2 ÷ 2 = 1
2 x 2 = 4		4 ÷ 2 = 2
3 x 2 = 6		6 ÷ 2 = 3
4 x 2 = 8		8 ÷ 2 = 4
5 x 2 = 10		10 ÷ 2 = 5
6 x 2 = 12		12 ÷ 2 = 6
7 x 2 = 14		14 ÷ 2 = 7
8 x 2 = 16		16 ÷ 2 = 8
9 x 2 = 18		18 ÷ 2 = 9
10 x 2 = 20		20 ÷ 2 = 10

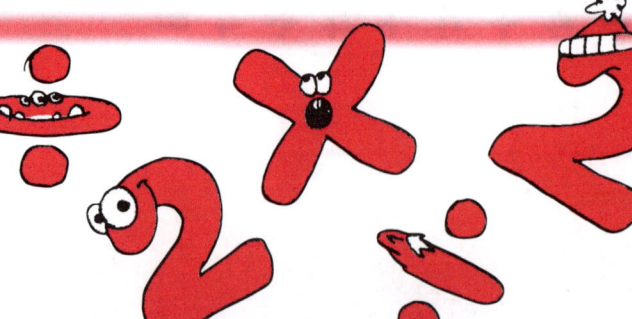

This activity will help your child to realise what multiplication and division facts mean.

Use real objects to demonstrate each fact so your child isn't just learning by rote.

Parents

Use the multiplication and division table to join the sums to their opposite partner with a line. The first has been done for you.

1 x 2 = 2   4 ÷ 2 = 2

5 x 2 = 10   2 ÷ 2 = 1

2 x 2 = 4   10 ÷ 2 = 5

3 x 2 = 6   8 ÷ 2 = 4

4 x 2 = 8   6 ÷ 2 = 3

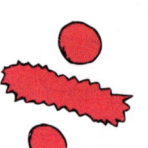
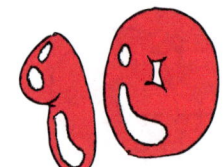

The 10 times table

Learn your table facts for the 10 times table using multiplication and division facts:

1 x 10 = 10	10 ÷ 10 = 1
2 x 10 = 20	20 ÷ 10 = 2
3 x 10 = 30	30 ÷ 10 = 3
4 x 10 = 40	40 ÷ 10 = 4
5 x 10 = 50	50 ÷ 10 = 5
6 x 10 = 60	60 ÷ 10 = 6
7 x 10 = 70	70 ÷ 10 = 7
8 x 10 = 80	80 ÷ 10 = 8
9 x 10 = 90	90 ÷ 10 = 9
10 x 10 = 100	100 ÷ 10 = 10

This activity will help your child to understand what their tables 'mean' rather than learning them by rote.

Use real objects to demonstrate each fact physically.

Use the multiplication and division table to join the banners to their opposite plane with a line.

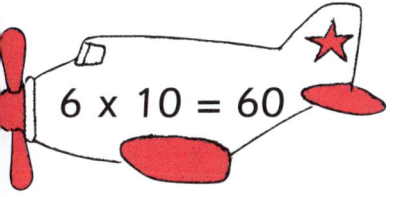

6 x 10 = 60

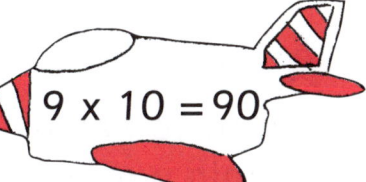

9 x 10 = 90

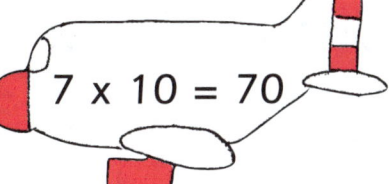

7 x 10 = 70

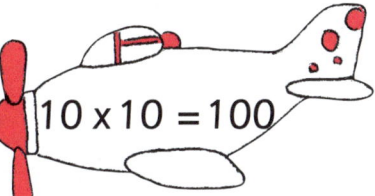

10 x 10 = 100

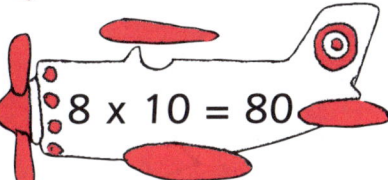

8 x 10 = 80

70 ÷ 10 = 7

90 ÷ 10 = 9

80 ÷ 10 = 8

60 ÷ 10 = 6

100 ÷ 10 = 10

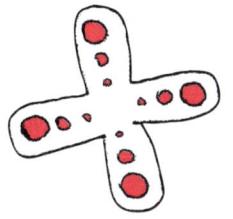

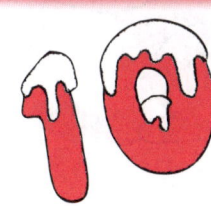

Multiplication turnaround

Here is a useful maths trick! When you multiply two numbers together, it does not matter in which order the numbers you are multiplying appear!

Look!

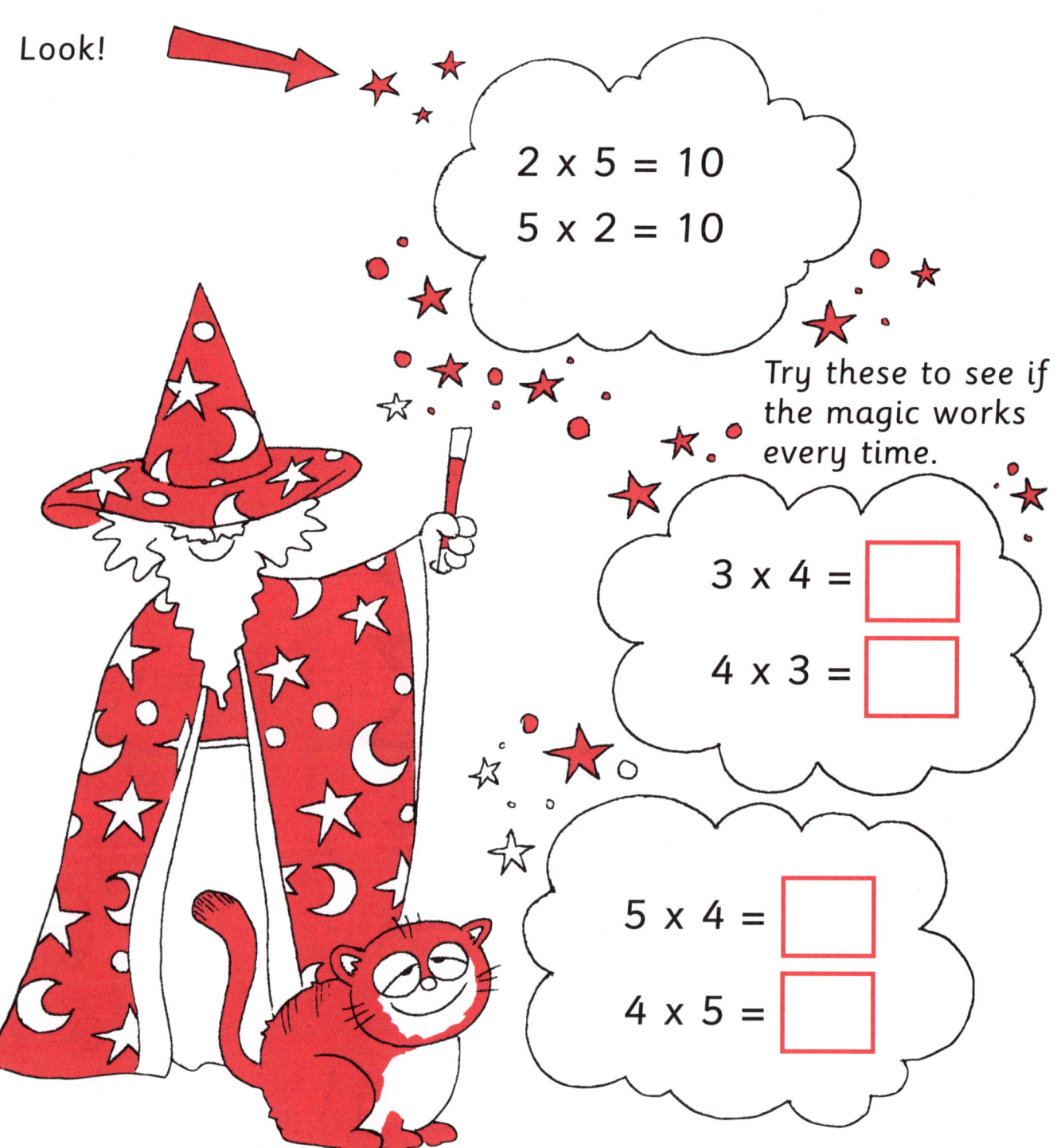

$2 \times 5 = 10$
$5 \times 2 = 10$

Try these to see if the magic works every time.

$3 \times 4 = \boxed{}$

$4 \times 3 = \boxed{}$

$5 \times 4 = \boxed{}$

$4 \times 5 = \boxed{}$

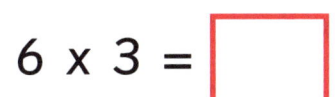

This activity will show your child that the order does not matter when multiplying.

Provide some examples to show that this is true for addition and multiplication but NOT for division and subtraction.

47

6 x 3 = ☐

3 x 6 = ☐

9 x 2 = ☐

2 x 9 = ☐

7 x 3 = ☐

3 x 7 = ☐

6 x 1 = ☐

1 x 6 = ☐

Remember, this rule only works for + and x and **not** for − and ÷.

10 x 3 = ☐

3 x 10 = ☐

8 x 2 = ☐

2 x 8 = ☐

41

The words of maths

Make a maths mobile!
Cut out rectangles of card and print these words carefully on the front and back. Ask someone to help you to make the mobile.

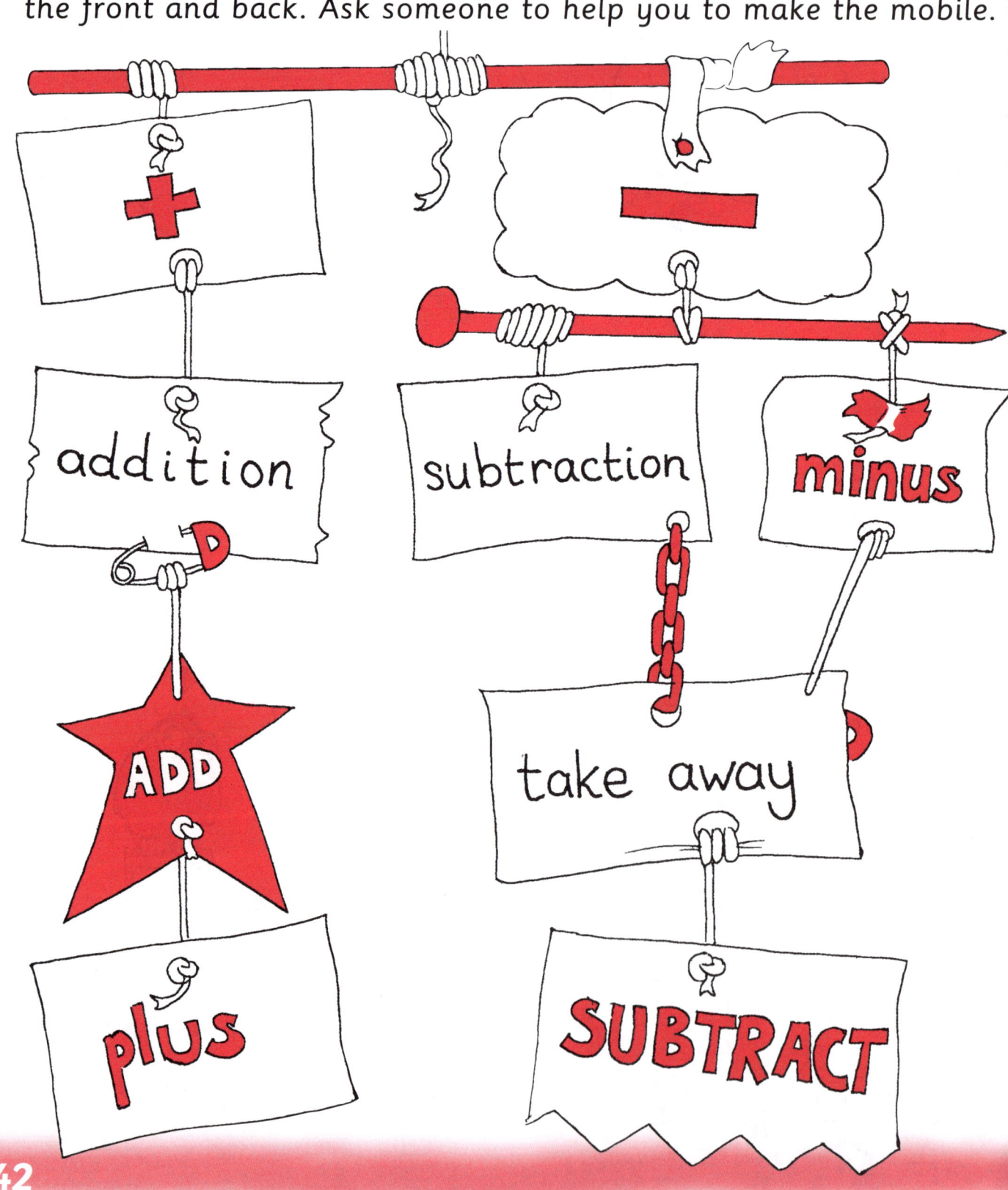

Parents

47

- This activity will help your child to associate maths language with its symbols.
- Help your child string the words for each symbol in a line below the symbol. Then hang the strings somewhere you can easily see them.

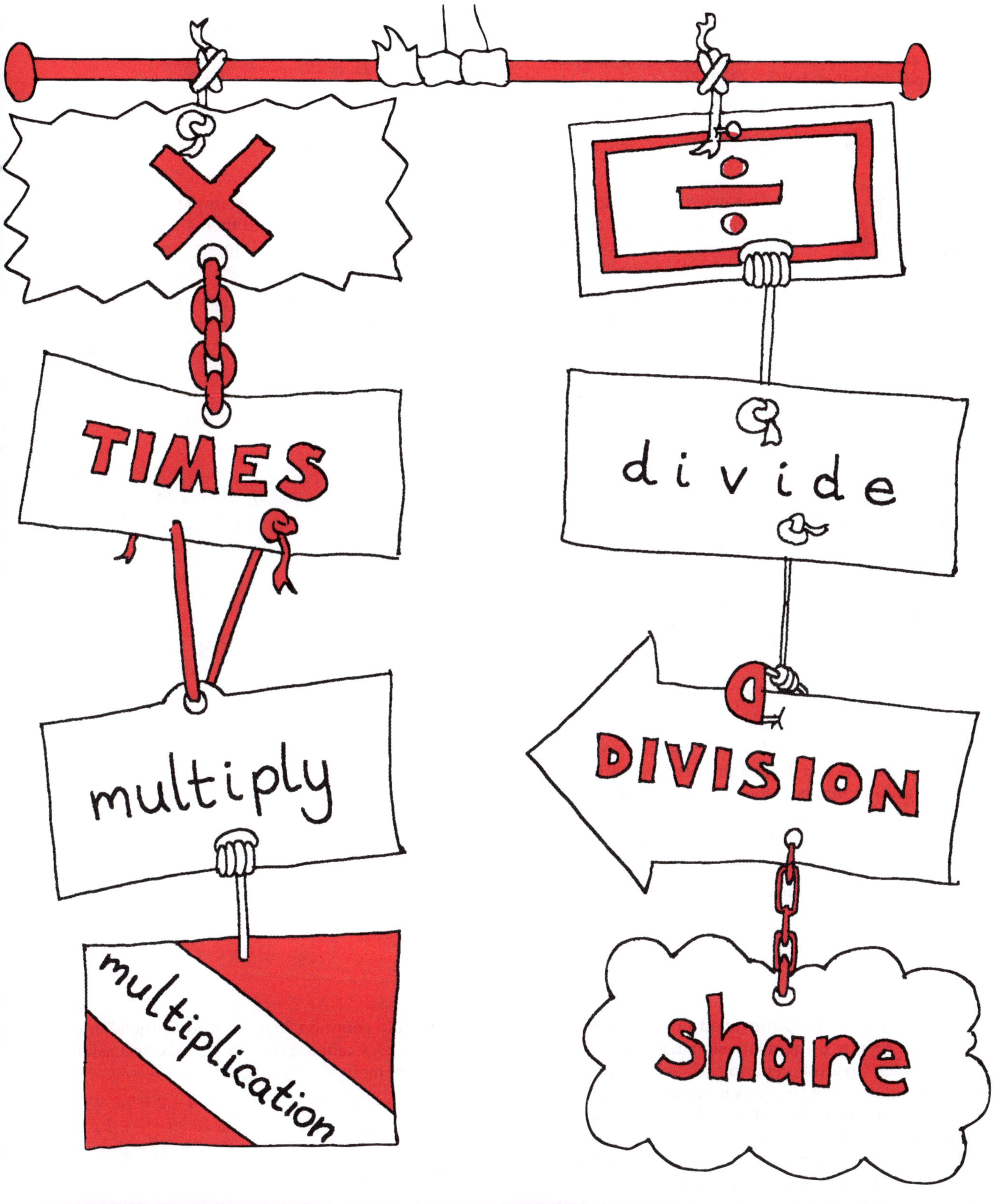

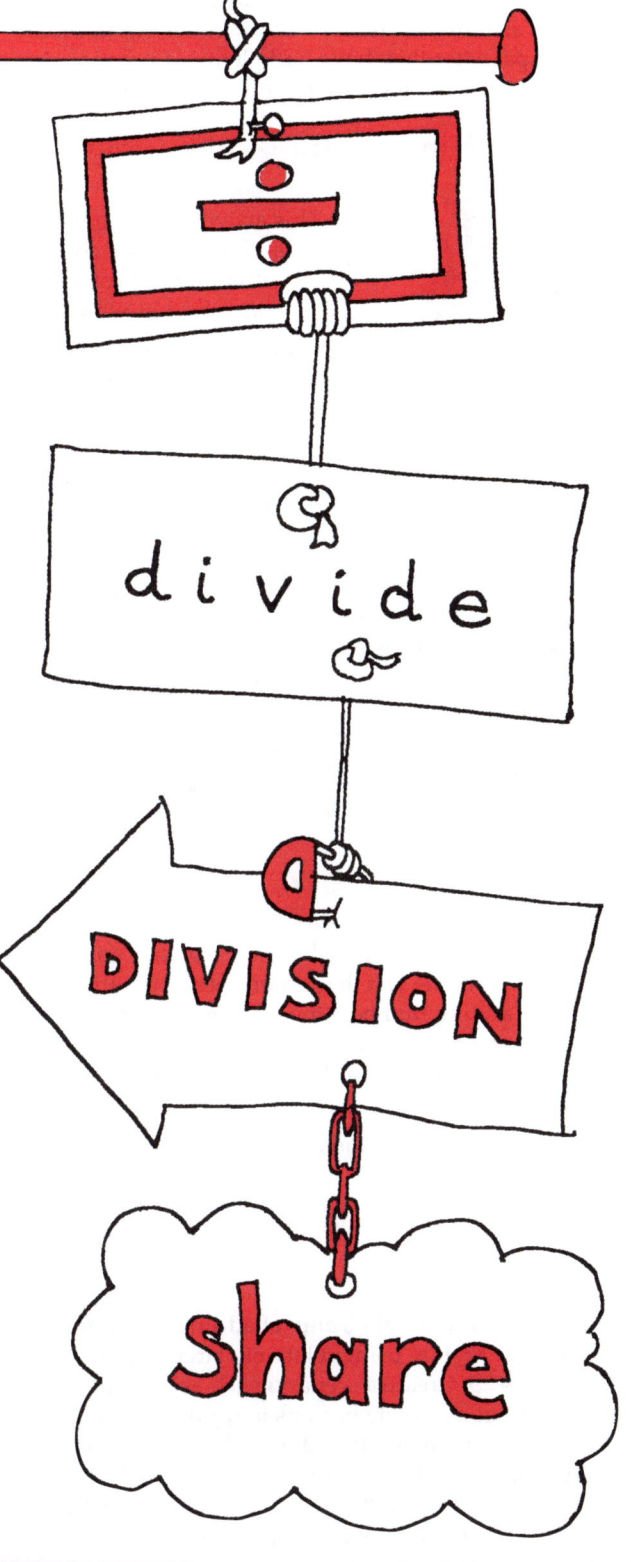

×
TIMES
multiply
multiplication
÷
divide
DIVISION
share

Further activities

To extend this activity, make up sets of three numbers for your child to add. Your child may find it easier initially to add these numbers by using 'concrete' materials, that is, actual objects such as buttons, shells or counters set out in three groups. After they have had plenty of practice, adding the numbers on paper will become easier.

▶ *Answers: 1. 10, 2. 14, 3. 12, 4. 10, 5. 14, 6. 13, 7. 14, 8. 11, 9. 10*

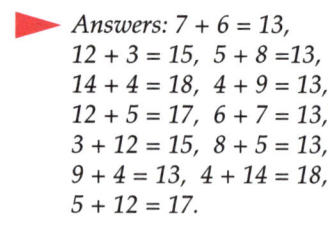

▶ This activity is designed to help your child to cope with number problems presented in words.

▶ You can develop the activity by asking your child similar questions in practical everyday contexts, for example, at the shops, ask, 'If we buy 3 apples and then 4 apples, how many apples do we have?' Compare quantities, using the terms 'more', 'less' and 'altogether'.

▶ *Answers: Shushi picked 14 flowers. Pat picked 13 flowers. Simon picked 27 pieces of fruit. Rosie picked 20 vegetables. Shushi picked more.*

▶ Practise this activity by 'counting on' with your child regularly, saying, for example, 'I have 3 cakes on this plate and 5 on this plate. How many do I have altogether?' Count on 5 from 3 to find the answer.

This may also be repeated with toys, books and clothing.

▶ *Answers: 4 + 12 = 16, 6 + 8 = 14, 13 + 7 = 20, 6 + 7 = 13, 17 + 3 = 20, 4 + 9 = 13, 2 + 8 = 10, 6 + 1 = 7, 1 + 6 = 7, 14 + 3 = 17, 9 + 2 = 11.*

▶ Adding groups of actual objects together will help to illustrate the fact that order does not matter when adding numbers together. Ask your child whether they will have more sweets if they add 3 sweets to 9 sweets, or 9 sweets to 3 sweets.

Check the answer by moving the groups of sweets and adding them together.

▶ *Answers: 7 + 6 = 13, 12 + 3 = 15, 5 + 8 =13, 14 + 4 = 18, 4 + 9 = 13, 12 + 5 = 17, 6 + 7 = 13, 3 + 12 = 15, 8 + 5 = 13, 9 + 4 = 13, 4 + 14 = 18, 5 + 12 = 17.*

▶ Show your child the value of adding the largest number first by using relatively large numbers, such as 25. Create a scenario such as needing to count out chocolate buttons to decorate cakes. Place 25 on one plate and 5 on the second plate. Ask your child to add the two quantities together. Firstly, give them the 5 buttons to count, then the 25. Write the numbers on a piece of paper. Ask them to count on 25 more from 5, then 5 more from 25. Compare the two results, and ask them which method was quicker.

▶ *Answers: 8 + 3 + 2 = 13, 12 + 4 + 2 = 18, 13 + 5 + 2 = 20, 9 + 7 + 2 = 18, 9 + 7 + 4 = 20, 12 + 8 + 2 = 22, 18 + 1 + 0 = 19, 17 + 3 + 0 = 20, 8 + 4 + 1 = 13, 11 + 8 + 5 = 24.*

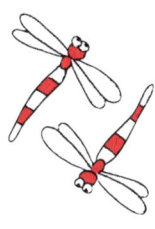

-15

▶ To extend this activity, make two sets of cards with number combinations that add together to make 10, for example, (0 + 10), (1 + 9), (2 + 8), (3 + 7), (4 + 6), (5 + 5), (6 + 4), (7 + 3), (8 + 2), (9 + 1), (10 + 0). Use these cards to play a variety of games which will familiarise your child with the number combinations; for example, 'Snap!' or 'Pelmanism'.

▶ *Answers: 2. 6 + 4 = 10 + 5 = 15,*
3. 5 + 5 = 10 + 9 = 19,
4. 3 + 7= 10 + 8 = 18,
5. 9 + 1 = 10 + 4 = 14,
6. 10 + 0 = 10 + 6 = 16,
7. 2 + 8 = 10 + 3 = 13,
8. 9 + 1 = 10 + 8 = 18,
9. 4 + 6 = 10 + 8 = 18.

-17

▶ Once again, you can make cards, as above, to familiarise your child with number combinations that make 20. You can also make cards that have one number of the pair on one side, and the corresponding number of the pair on the other side. Your child should choose a card and try to remember the other half of the pair. They can check the answer by turning over the card.

▶ *Answers: 1. 8 + 12, 7 + 13, 11 + 9, 10 + 10, 9 + 11.*
2. 0 + 20, 3 + 17, 1 + 19, 4 + 16, 2 + 18, 5 + 15,
6 + 14. 3. 12 + 8, 13 + 7, 14 + 6, 15 + 5, 16 + 4,
17 + 3. 4. 19 + 1, 18 + 2, 20 + 0.

-19

▶ You might make a game of saying a number – a multiple of 10 to 100 for instance – and your child has to say the corresponding number to make a total of 100. Point out the similarity between numbers that combine to make a total of 10 and numbers that combine to make a total of 100, for instance, 1 and 9 and 10 and 90, 2 and 8 and 20 and 80, 3 and 7 and 30 and 70. Point out the only difference in the written number is the zero.

▶ *Answers: 10 + 90, 0 + 100, 100 + 0,*
20 + 80, 70 + 30, 50 + 50, 40 + 60,
90 + 10, 30 + 70, 80 + 20, 60 + 40.

-21

▶ Invent 'number stories' of your own – they could be about family members, pets or toys. Write the stories out with your child, perhaps making books out of A4 paper to record the stories. These may be illustrated by your child, or by cutting pictures from magazines, or using photographs.

▶ *Answers: 7 spiders – 3 spiders = 4 spiders,*
6 snails + 5 snails = 11 snails,
11 snails – 5 snails = 6 snails,
9 centipedes + 1 centipede = 10 centipedes,
10 centipedes – 1 centipede = 9 centipedes,
6 dragonflies + 2 dragonflies = 8 dragonflies,
8 dragonflies – 2 dragonflies = 6 dragonflies,
4 beetles + 3 beetles = 7 beetles,
7 beetles – 3 beetles = 4 beetles.

-23

▶ Extend this activity by practising inverse operations with your child in practical contexts. Show them, for example, that subtraction after an addition will take you back to where you started. Say 'I have 3 plums in this hand and 4 plums in this hand. How many plums do I have altogether?' When your child has added the total by counting on, say 'Yes, I have 7 plums altogether. If I take away 4 plums, how many will I have altogether? Yes, I shall have 3 plums – I'm back where I started!' This can be repeated with many other scenarios.

▶ *Answers: 3 + 6 = 9 9 – 6 = 3, 6 + 1 = 7 7 – 1 = 6,*
4 + 6 = 10 10 – 6 = 4, 9 + 3 = 12 12 – 3 = 9,
5 + 2 = 7 7 – 2 = 5, 7 + 5 = 12 12 – 5 = 7,
15 + 5 = 20 20 – 5 = 15, 13 + 7 = 20 20 – 7 = 13,
11 + 6 = 17 17 – 6 = 11, 19 + 1 = 20 20 – 1 = 19,
14 + 3 = 17 17 – 3 = 14, 12 + 4 = 16 16 – 4 = 12.

Further activities

24–25

▶ Help your child to understand these 'number families', by making up your own sets of calculations. You could even draw a picture together of a family of 4 – it could be monsters, aliens, animals or people – with the calculations on their hats. If you put the picture on the wall somewhere your child will see regularly, it will help them to remember their 'number families'.

▶ *Answers: 3 + 5 = 8*
8 – 3 = 5, 8 – 5 = 3,
9 + 6 = 15 15 – 9 = 6
15 – 6 = 9, 5 + 14 = 19
19 – 5 = 14 19 – 14 = 5.

26–27

▶ Set up a game to play 'The Great Zero Game Show' with your child. Use toy cars or teddies as the 'prizes' and take turns with your child being the contestant and the quizmaster. Ask questions such as, 'I have 4 toy cars. If I add 0 cars, how many will

I have? Yes, 4! If I take away 0 cars, how many will I have? Yes, 4! We have another winner!' Make the game fun, with lots of cheering and clapping. If your child enjoys themselves, they are more likely to remember.

▶ *Answers: 18 + 0 = 18, 24 + 0 = 24, 30 + 0 = 30*
18 – 0 = 18, 24 – 0 = 24, 30 – 0 = 30.

28–29

▶ To help your child to understand division as sharing, give them lots of practical experience such as sharing out sweets, grapes or toys.

▶ Ask your child to estimate the number of items each person will receive. Talk about 'dividing' items amongst people, and write the practical problem down in 'maths language'. For example, say 'We need to share

6 biscuits among 3 people, so that is 6 divided by 3'.

▶ *Answers: 9, 3, 10, 2, 8, 6, 1, 9, 5, 7, 4, 9.*
18 ÷ 2 = 9, 10 ÷ 2 = 5, 24 ÷ 2 = 12,
6 ÷ 2 = 3, 8 ÷ 2 = 4, 12 ÷ 2 = 6,
14 ÷ 2 = 7, 10 ÷ 2 = 5, 16 ÷ 2 = 8.

30–31

▶ Carry out practical examples of division as grouping objects. Put a pile of 20 sweets on the table and say, 'I have 20 sweets. I need to share them into 4 groups of 5 so that everyone gets a fair share'. Ask your child to group the sweets. Carry out other grouping activities in the same way.

▶ *Answers: Check your child has joined the labels to the correct baskets.*

32–33

▶ In the same way as for the previous activity, carry out practical grouping activites to help your child to develop confidence with

division. Make up questions such as 'If there are 8 scones and I put 2 on each plate, how many plates will I need?'

▶ *Answers: 6 ÷ 2 = 3, 20 ÷ 5 = 4, 16 ÷ 2 = 8,*
15 ÷ 3 = 5, 18 ÷ 6 = 3, 12 ÷ 2 = 6, 25 ÷ 5 = 5,
15 ÷ 3 = 5, 18 ÷ 3 = 6, 9 ÷ 3 = 3, 24 ÷ 3 = 8.

▶ Use items such as shells, pine cones and acorns to demonstrate that multiplication is another way of expressing repeated addition – that is 3 + 3 + 3 = 9 is the same as 3 x 3 = 9. Both calculations are finding the total of '3 lots of 3'. Lay out items to show this.

▶ *Answers: 3 + 3 + 3 = 9   3 x 3 = 9,*
5 + 5 + 5 + 5 = 20   5 x 4 = 20,
6 + 6 + 6 = 18   6 x 3 = 18,
4 + 4 + 4 = 12   4 x 3 = 12,
5 + 5 + 5 = 15   5 x 3 = 15,
3 + 3 + 3 + 3 + 3 = 15   3 x 5 = 15,
6 + 6 + 6 + 6 = 24   6 x 4 = 24
4 + 4 + 4 + 4 + 4 + 4 + 4 = 28   4 x 7 = 28.

▶ *Answers: 1 x 2 = 2 and 2 ÷ 2 = 1,*
5 x 2 = 10 and 10 ÷ 2 = 5,
2 x 2 = 4 and 4 ÷ 2 = 2,
3 x 2 = 6 and 6 ÷ 2 = 3,
4 x 2 = 8 and 8 ÷ 2 = 4.

▶ To help your child to learn these multiplication and division facts, make sets of cards as follows: a set of cards with the multiplication question on one side, say '5 x 2' and the answer on the other, in this case '10'.

In each case, the child uses the cards to test themselves because the answer is available on the reverse of the card.

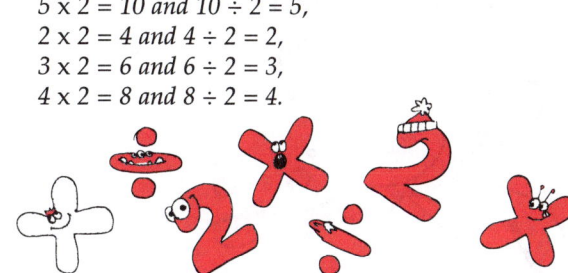

▶ To help your child to learn these multiplication and division facts, make sets of cards as follows: a set of cards with the division question on one side, say '30 ÷ 10' and the answer on the other, in this case '3'.

You might also make a set of cards with a multiplication on one side and the corresponding division on the other, for instance '1 x 10 = 10' and '10 ÷ 10 = 1'. In each case, the child uses the cards to test themselves because the answer is available on the reverse of the card.

▶ *Answers: 6 x 10 = 60 and 60 ÷ 10 = 6, 9 x 10 = 90 and 90 ÷ 10 = 9, 70 ÷ 10 = 7 and 7 x 10 = 70, 10 x 10 = 100 and 100 ÷ 10 = 10, 8 x 10 = 80 and 80 ÷ 10 = 8.*

▶ Help your child to understand that order does not matter in addition and multiplication calculations by practising both with actual objects and on paper. It is important to point out that order DOES matter with subtraction and division. Point this out with practical examples such as, 'Take 3 cakes away from 4 cakes and then try to take 4 cakes away from 3 cakes'. Children of this age need not to be concerned with negative or minus numbers, so tell them simply that you are unable to take 4 away from 3.

▶ *Answers: 3 x 4 = 12 4 x 3 = 12, 5 x 4 = 20 4 x 5 = 20, 6 x 3 = 18 3 x 6 = 18, 9 x 2 = 18 2 x 9 = 18, 7 x 3 = 21 3 x 7 = 21, 6 x 1 = 6 1 x 6 = 6, 10 x 3 = 30 3 x 10 = 30, 8 x 2 = 16 2 x 8 = 16.*

▶ To extend this activity, make a set of cards (paper will suffice) with the vocabulary words and symbols written on. Make 20 more cards of the same size with a picture on. Use the cards to play 'Happy Families' where the 'family' in each case is, for example, all the words meaning 'add'.

Celebration!

You are so clever!
Colour the stars to show
what you can do!

I can add by counting on.

I can add all the pairs of numbers that make
10, 20 and 100.

I can subtract, divide and multiply.

I know my 2 and 10 times table.